Count Your Way through Russia

947

DATE DUE

Carolrhoda Books, Inc./Minneapolis

To Elisa Beth and the future

Text copyright © 1987 by Jim Haskins
Illustrations copyright © 1987 by Carolrhoda Books, Inc.

This book is available in two editions:
Library binding by Carolrhoda Books, Inc.
Soft cover by First Avenue Editions
c/o The Lerner Group
241 First Avenue North
Minneapolis, Minnesota 55401

LIBRARY OF CONGRESS CATALOGING-IN-PUBLICATION DATA

Haskins, James, 1941-
    Count your way through Russia.

    Summary: Presents the numbers one through ten in
Russian, using each number to introduce concepts about
the Soviet Union and Russian culture.
    1. Soviet Union—Juvenile literature.   2. Counting—
Juvenile literature.   [1. Soviet Union.   2. Counting]
I. Mednikov, Vera, ill.   II. Title.
DK43.H39   1987   947   87-6397
ISBN 0-87614-303-6 (lib bdg.)
ISBN 0-87614-488-1 (pbk.)

Manufactured in the United States of America

        7   8   9 10 – P/SP – 01 00 99 98 97 96 95 94

Introductory Note

The Russian language, like the English language, has one alphabet. This alphabet, called the Cyrillic alphabet, has 33 letters, which are used to form all Russian words. The Russian language uses Arabic numerals for its number system, as do many other languages, including English.

Russia is the largest country in the world in land area. From 1922 to 1991, Russia was part of the Soviet Union, which was made up of 15 different republics. The Soviet Union broke up in 1991, and Russia and some of the other republics formed the Commonwealth of Independent States. Each of these states is an independent country. Russian was the official language of the Soviet Union, and it is now the official language of Russia.

ОДИН ○ **1** ○ (ah-DEEN)

There is only **one** Kremlin, and it is the most famous group of buildings in Russia. The Kremlin is located in Moscow and is the center of government for Russia. It began as a wooden fortress in 1156, and what stands today is the result of centuries of continual construction and rebuilding. The 66-acre enclosed area includes magnificent cathedrals, monasteries, palaces, a theater, a museum, and a modern office building. Many of Russia's most valuable artistic and historical treasures are kept in the Kremlin.

ДВА ● **2** ● **(dvah)**

Two snowshoes are needed for walking outside during the long winters of the northwestern, central, and eastern parts of Russia. These areas have snow and ice for many months of the year. Around the White Sea, winter lasts for about nine months, and far northern Siberia has ice and snow for ten months of each year.

ТРИ  **3** (tree)

Troika (TROY-kuh) is a Russian word meaning a group of **three**. A Russian sleigh drawn by three horses that are side by side is called a *troika*.

ЧЕТЫРЕ ● **4** ● (chih-TEE-reh)

Russia has more land area than any other country in the world. In fact, it is almost twice the size of Canada, the second largest country. It takes **four** days to go just halfway across Russia on the Trans-Siberian Express train.

ПЯТЬ  5 (pyaht)

It takes **five** people to dance the *Pereplyas* (pare-uh-plee-us), a popular folk dance in Russia. The name *Pereplyas* means to dance longer and better than others. The five people try to outdo each other in skill and in making up new steps.

The dancers wear their national costume, which usually consists of an embroidered shirt and trousers that are tucked into black boots.

ШЕСТЬ 6 **(shayst)**

Six times in a row, from 1964 to 1984, Russian couples won the Olympic gold medal for pairs figure skating. These athletes spent long hours training to be the best in their sport.

СЕМЬ **7** **(seeaym)**

The number **seven** is very important in Russian culture. There are seven domes on churches and seven bells in bell towers. One of the most popular items of Russian folk art is the set of seven nesting dolls called *Matryoshka* (mah-tree-OSH-kuh). Each doll fits inside the next until they are all inside of the seventh and largest doll.

ВОСЕМЬ  (VOH-seeaym)

For Russian women, the number **eight** is especially important. On March 8 each year, Russia celebrates Women's Day. Schools and offices are closed for the day, and many women receive flowers from their families.